The

Money

Field

Book 2

Money Goals and Money Management Tools

Nelson Letshwene

Your Money Trees and Money Management Tools

Money Goals and Money Management Tools

Your Money Trees and Money Management Tools

Practical Strategies for Living in the Gap

Nelson Letshwene

The Money Field Series – Book 2

Copyright©2020 R. Nelson Letshwene

All rights reserved. This book is intellectual property protected by international copyright law. No part of this publication may be reproduced in any form without the prior written permission of the author and publisher, except in brief quotations embodied in critical articles and reviews.

Published by Moedi Publishing
Gaborone, Botswana. Pretoria, South Africa
©2020 R. Nelson Letshwene
PO BOX 80927, Gaborone, Botswana
PO Box 1766 Rustenburg, South Africa
nelslets@gmail.com / nelson@moedi.net
www.nelsonletshwene.com
Moedi Publishing
ISBN: 978-0-9870189-0-8

KDP ISBN
979-8741408896

Money Goals and Money Management Tools

> *"Until you accomplish a thing harmoniously, it's never permanently done;*
> *And as long as you fight a thing, it will fight you back"*
>
> Saint Germain

DISCLAIMER:

This publication is designed to provide competent and reliable general information regarding the subject matter covered. However, it is published with the understanding that the author and publisher are not engaged in rendering legal, financial, or other professional advice. If legal, financial, or other expert assistance is required, the services of a professional should be sought. The author and publisher specifically disclaim any liability that is incurred from the use or application of the contents of this book.

Table of Contents

DISCLAIMER: vii
INTRODUCTION TO BOOK 2 x
THE MONEY MANAGEMENT MODEL 1
1. LIVING IN THE GAP 5
   What are the implications of living in this gap?.. 7
      The Psychology of reaching goals 9
2. BUDGETING PRINCIPLES 11
   The Budget Spending Sheet 12
   Your Annual Budget Principles: 14
      Commitment 17
      Principles 19
3. PRINCIPLES OF SAVING 27
   Pay yourself first 28
   Your Money's Friends and Foes 30
   Funding your emergencies 34
4. YOUR PERSONAL MONEY TREE 41
   How do you find your own Money Tree? 43
   Personal Skills Inventory 48
5. MARKETING YOUR PERSONAL SKILLS 53
   Who Has Money to Give You? 54
      Who Has Vested Interest? 58
6. HOME, SWEET HOME! 61
   Start Early 63
   The buyer's Checklist 65
7. INFORMATION – THE PAPER TRAIL 71
      Information Gathering: 74
      Classification of Information 77

8. PHYSICAL ARRANGEMENT OF INFORMATION 81
Choosing an Accounting Period 86
Information-Gathering Sheet 87

9. CREATING RECORDS 91
Bank Reconciliation Statement 93
Cheque Book Balancing 94
Section A: Income And Expense Statement 95
Section B: Statement of Cash Flow 96
Section C: Balance Sheet 97

10. A JOURNEY OF DISCOVERY 100
SECTION A: INCOME 102
SECTION B: EXPENSES 111

11. MY NET WORTH – WHAT HAS MY MONEY DONE FOR ME? 125
SUMMARY 138

ACKNOWLEDGEMENTS 140

About the Author 143

BIBLIOGRAPHY 144
For More books by Nelson Letshwene 147

INTRODUCTION TO BOOK 2

The Money Field is a three-book series that started with *How to Set Your Own Money Rules;* has progressed to this Your *Money Trees and Money Management Tools - Practical Strategies for Living in the Gap*, and will close with *How to Pay Off Your Debt and Build Wealth - Debt Management Principles* in book three.

All these areas are put together in one book in the print version as part one, part two and part three.

While it would be helpful to read book one in the series, the topics in this book are stand-alone topics and you will still learn a lot just by reading this book. You will not necessarily be disadvantaged if you have not read the first book in the series, although it is strongly recommended that you do for the sake of the foundational framework that the first book sets. Some of the material in this book was formerly published in the book *Functional Mastery Over My Finances* (Reach publishers, 2008). Although some of the chapters that formed that book are in this book, they have been revamped, improved, updated, edited and made better for the sake of this new book series; and many other chapters of that book have been excluded.

I hope this book series will add value to the life of the reader, and help to increase financial literacy and other money skills that are so important in our lives today.

If you find this book helpful, feel free to give us some feedback or leave us a review for further improvements.

Thank you,

Nelson Letshwene

April, 2021
Gaborone, Botswana

PREFACE

THE MONEY MANAGEMENT MODEL

"Honesty is a very expensive gift. Do not expect it from cheap people."
Warren Buffet

If you have had opportunity to have read the first book in the series, you would have experienced the money management model we call The Money Field.

This money management model that facilitates the money game, is a four-quadrant system that tracks your money from the time that it enters the income quadrant, and follows it all around The Money Field. It tracks money from the income quadrant to the various areas and categories of the expenses quadrant. It further tracks how money may leave "other people's pockets", to come into your pockets and form obligations in your liabilities quadrant.

From your income quadrant, your main focus is to grow your asset quadrant. Financial success is often measured by the size of your asset quadrant, continually fed and supported by your income quadrant.

The two quadrants that take money away from you are the expenses quadrant and the liabilities quadrant, which reduces your net worth.

In this second book of the series, we focus on "practical strategies for living in the gap".

"The Gap" is the distance between your current state and your desired state. In the game of money, you are always in transition from one state to another. You may be transitioning from low income to high income through strategies of multiple streams of income. This book has chapters that focus on those strategies.

You also need strategies of protection and sustenance. You will also encounter practical money management tools such as budgeting, and principles of increase like savings and investments.

In Practical Strategies for Living in the Gap, you will experience the real work that goes with money management. You will be challenged to employ the tools that are important in the physical management of your money. You are encouraged to either draw the tools in your private workbooks, or download spreadsheets that will get you involved in the real game of managing and taking control of your finances.

Chapter 1

1. LIVING IN THE GAP

"We devour the bread of charity because we are hungry; it revives, then slays us."

Kahlil Gibran

LEARNING OUTCOMES

In this chapter you will learn:

- The implications of living in the gap
- Tools for living in the gap
- The psychology of reaching goals

A GAP is the distance between your current state and the state you will be in when your goal is achieved.

The setting of any goal creates a gap between where you are and where you intend to be. Managing this gap is what will determine whether you reach your goals or not. People fail to reach their goals only because they don't perceive the gap between where they are and where they want to go.

If you can know exactly where you are beginning, and perceive the distance where you are going, you have to get ready to live in the gap. It is vitally important to practically define the implications of your goals on your current life. You will have to change something and maintain the change until you reach your goals. When you say you want to lose weight because you like the new fashion that's out there, it does not mean if you went and bought small size clothes tomorrow you will be slim. There is a gap between where you are and where you want to go. Can you live in this gap?

What are the implications of living in this gap?

Once a goal is set, it will not achieve itself. A financial goal often implies a change in current lifestyle until the goal is reached.

If you are not someone who is accustomed to saving money, and now you decide that saving is going to be one of your goals, you must understand that the money that you want to start saving, will have to come from somewhere, which implies that some other area of your life will have to change. You have to choose what that area is, make adjustments, and commit.

You are either going to cut on something to save the money, or you are going to start doing something to generate the extra cash that you want to save. If you don't want to go out and make extra money, then you must learn about budgeting, and choose to cut something out.

The trouble with many people is that they want to have their cake and eat it. If you have identified your 'eating-out' money as the portion of your money that you would now like to put into savings, you must understand that now you have to cut down on eating out. This is where strict adherence to a tool called a budget may become useful.

If your goal is to get out of debt, you must understand that continuing to live on the credit card or on revolving credit is not going to work. You have to stop borrowing completely, and perhaps realise that your gap includes making more money to cover the existing debt.

A budget is a tool that will help you to live in the gap. A debt management program is a tool you could employ to live in the gap. A weight management program is a tool that has to be your companion as you live in your gap.

If your goal is to be rich, then your gap will involve a wealth growing tool that you are applying as you live in your gap. But it has to be a wealth generating tool. The gap is not just a practical place, but it is also a psychological place. It speaks well of your commitment to your ideals. If you are committed to your WHY, your HOW will come easy.

The Psychology of reaching goals

Most goals, if not well calculated and thought out, can be daunting and therefore discouraging. You need to break your goals down into manageable chunks. It is important to know exactly where you are, exactly where you are going, and manage the gap in between.

SELF-ASSESSMENT

1. What does it mean to live in the gap?

2. What tools do you need to be able to live successfully in the gap?

3. What, according to you, is the best way to implement your "gap-strategy"?

4. What are some of the psychological issues associated with living in the gap?

Chapter 2

2. BUDGETING PRINCIPLES

The habit of saving is itself an education; it fosters every virtue, teaches self-denial, cultivates the sense of order, trains to forethought, and so broadens the mind.

T.T. Munger

LEARNING OUTCOMES
- What is a budget
- Budgeting principles
- How to create a budgeting worksheet
- How to draw an annual budget
- The importance of commitment

Money Goals and Money Management Tools

The Budget Spending Sheet

The trouble with so many people, is that they've never taken the time to understand what proper financial planning is all about. They always assumed they know, until they are in trouble. At the end of every month, there's that little sheet that comes out called a budget.

The biggest trouble is not that they don't want to plan, but the truth is they don't know what a budget is.

- They think by writing out an expense sheet every month that they are 'budgeting'. Can you imagine if the government did that? Do you see the minister of finance looking at how much VAT was collected this month, and then, and only then deciding what will be paid this month? (Would your salary be

covered if you worked for government – you would wonder!) It's ridiculous. Yet, that's what many of us do every month.
- This "monthly budgeting" leads to increased frustration because it doesn't work.
  - That's why most of us toss it out the window and go to the loan sharks to borrow survival money.
  - That's why our credit cards are maxed to the limit.
  - That's why that squeaky bed and ragged sofa have not been replaced yet … it's because they never made it on the real budget three years ago …because there was no budget …no foresight!

A budget must be done <u>ONCE</u> a year, and it must include two to five-year planning in it. What you do every month, is monitoring, not 'budgeting'. A budget gives you a chance to decide how much money you *want* to make, and what you *want* to save and spend for that year. It is not necessarily based on what you already have, but it gives you a chance to grow. Most people have been living day to day for a long time. If they don't change this day-to-day living mentality, this will go on until retirement. They have set themselves up to fail ...

You might say, but I only have one job and it only pays me so much. Well, if what they pay you is enough to meet your long-term budget, good. If not, have you heard of the saying: 'think outside the box'?

To think outside the box, you must first determine what has been boxing you in. What limitations have you subscribed to? So, what should you do?

Your Annual Budget

Principles:

First, make a list of everything you would like

to achieve this financial year. A financial year may be the same as a calendar year, or it may start as a twelve months cycle from wherever you are. Some people choose their birth month as the first month of their planning year.

Draw a full year calendar and put it in front of you. You may have Quarterly totals for each quarter (Q1 – Q4)

JANUARY	FEBRUARY	MARCH	Q1
APRIL	MAY	JUNE	Q2
JULY	AUGUST	SEPTEMBER	Q3
OCTOBER	NOVEMBER	DECEMBER	Q4

Notice that each month of the year is financially unlike any other month. Notice the things that will happen only in those specific months and how those will affect your finances.

For example, Valentine's day will only happen in February; Easter will happen in April; Christmas will happen only in December. If you have school-going children, note the months in which you have to pay school fees. Notice months of family birthdays or family events. Notice your national calendar and see how national holidays affect your budget.

Now include all the fixed expenses that will happen every month of the year without variation. For example, your mortgage repayments or your rental is a constant figure all year round.

Now include your variable expenses on your budget. Be aware of seasonal differences. For example, your electricity bill will differ between summer and winter.

Take your time and include in your annual budget everything that you believe will happen this year, and what you would like to happen.

Add up all the costs for the year and see your total for the year. Now add up your projected income for the year. What is the difference between the projected expenses and the projected income? Do you have a deficit or a surplus budget?

If it's a deficit, what can you do now, before the year begins, to bridge the gap. What income producing projects can you initiate early on in the year?

If it's a surplus, what other investments can you think about?

Commitment

Tuberculosis (TB) is a curable disease, but the regiment is a long-term process. You have to take the medication for at least six months in most cases. You can't stop when you feel better after three months. If you don't take your medicine to the bitter end, you do get the bitter end, so to speak.

What is the point of going to the doctor if you are not going to take the prescription medicine?

Many of us approach our finances like an ill-disciplined TB patient. We stop when we feel better!

You must commit and reap the benefits of a changed financial future, or, if you don't commit, you go on with your life and never know the difference.

Why is it that most people don't keep a budget? There are various reasons: 'I don't make enough money to be on a budget', or 'Budgets are too restrictive', or 'I'm not good with numbers', or 'I am too ashamed because it exposes my ill-discipline with money.'

Well, for whatever reason you may not keep a budget, you are missing out on the possibilities of Financial Intelligence that you could develop as a result of understanding your finances.

As I have said before and will probably say it again: what you don't know about money will hurt you. So as far as money is concerned, ignorance is not bliss. The belief that a person does not have enough money to be on a budget indicates that the person does not understand the concept of budgeting.

Anyone with any amount of income, even a student, can create a simple budget that works, even as simple as the envelope method.

People on low incomes are probably in the greatest need of a budget to allow themselves to initiate new income producing projects early on in the year to improve their incomes.

Be aware that perhaps the most common budget error is simple discouragement. Remember, if your budget doesn't work the first month you try it, don't become discouraged. Developing a realistic budget takes time. Habits change slowly, especially spending habits.

It may take three to six months or more before your budget begins to work well, (especially if you have a lot of debt to deal with. See Debt Management section).

Principles

- Guard your money. Don't waste it. Every time you spend your money ask yourself: 'is this expense helping me to achieve my financial goals?' If the answer is 'yes', go ahead and spend, if the answer is 'no', think twice ... and empower yourself!
- A budget allows you to take control of your finances. A budget gives you the ability to plan ahead. You make conscious decisions about how to spend your money, instead of spending on impulse.
- Beware of the 'more-money-in, more-money-out' syndrome. This means you spend more simply because you have more. This is particularly dangerous if the extra money is temporary income. Just because you've got a salary increment does not mean you need to alter your spending habits. You could just invest the money for the future.
- If you earn on commission or are self-employed and therefore face a fluctuating income, you are more at risk of this

syndrome if you don't use a budget. So, take charge of your finances by determining your monthly averages quickly and prescribing a budget that will work for you.

Prioritize and categorise

Well, how do you start? Prioritise! First things first. You need to identify your living expenses.
- You need to pay Rent, (you can't live on someone else's money);
- Utilities (gas, water, electricity, - otherwise you'll be caught in the dark, cold and thirsty)
- Transportation (fuel, taxi/bus fare) If you have a car, include in this category your car insurance, and maintenance.
- Food – watch this spot, you can save a lot by eating at home or carrying your lunch pack and avoiding junk food. Childcare if you have kids. Telephone bill(s).

Next, begin a simple form of budget by dividing your actual income among predetermined priorities.

Then create a register or schedule for each priority (account).

Next divide your earnings among your priority accounts and enter each amount as a deposit in that account. You may use an envelope to separate the cash, or to separate the receipts each time you swipe your card.

Keep adding the amounts on these receipts to make sure that you don't exceed your allocated amount per category.

Finally, when you take money from that account, enter the transaction as a withdrawal from that account.

Don't forget the big question: 'is this expense helping me to achieve my financial goals?'

Don't pass up this opportunity to focus your financial resources on what is really important to you. It's well worth the time investment.

Keep receipts. Balance your cheque book regularly. Account for the ATM withdrawals.

Check your bank statement for debit orders and stop orders to make sure they have gone through, so that you don't get that surprise call demanding payment.

Take control of your money through the power of a budget! Budgeting gives you the power to control your financial future. With a budget you are able to set goals and go after them.

For most people, the future is not what it used to be. But with a budget and proper planning, the future can start looking bright again.

If you fail to plan, you have planned to fail! Having said all that, it is actually a whole lot easier to go make extra money than to try to live a restricted life.

We human beings are freedom seeking beings not prison seeking. We want to grow, not shrink.

When you think about your income, you might realise that most of it comes from a sale of only one skill that you have.

The truth is, you have a whole lot of other skills that you are currently not selling. In the chapter on The Money Tree, we will talk about how to identify more of your skills and how to sell more of them for your expanded self.

Your budget on the Money field:

Income budget o How much money would you like to make? o What is your plan	**Expenses Budget** o Set category limits o Set total expense limits
Asset Budget o Your security assets o Your investment assets	**Liabilities Budget** o What is the monthly limit from your salary that should go to service debt? o Which categories of debt are you working with?

SELF-ASSESSMENT

1. State some budgeting principles that you would like to apply

2. Highlight the difference between a budget and a spending sheet?

3. What is the importance of an annual budget?

4. How would an annual budget help you to think big?

Chapter 3

3. PRINCIPLES OF SAVING

"Growth investors will only play in opportunities that have consistent, above average returns …Income investors are looking for immediate cash out in the form of rental, lease, interest, or dividends payment"

Loral Langemeier

LEARNING OUTCOMES

In this chapter you will learn:

1. The principles of saving
2. The Pay Yourself First principle
3. Your money's friends and foes
4. How to fund your emergencies

After we discoursed on budgeting principles, the next big question may be Savings Principles. We've already discoursed on reasons why it is difficult to save in chapter 9. Now we should look to make it work. This may not be as easy as it may sound.

To build a strong house, you need a strong foundation. If you build on sand, the wind and the storms will beat against your house and it may fall with a big crash. Building a strong financial house needs you to understand the fundamentals first. Getting out of consumer debt and simultaneously paying yourself first must be your priority.

Pay yourself first

Starting the habit of paying yourself first is important, not so much for the amount of money you can actually save, but for the psychological advantage of developing a very important habit. Trying to save while you are in uncontrolled debt may of course seem counterproductive.

Of course, debt costs you more than what your money will make in a savings account. Banks and other lenders collect a lot of interest from you, even up to 30% depending on the product you are using as well as your credit rating, while they only give you between 1% and 7%, for deposits you make with them, also depending on the package and the amount of your deposit. Of course, these vary from economy to economy.

While I strongly recommend that you consult with a trusted financial advisor on your personal financial matters, my simple advice would be to understand the kind of debt that you are carrying, and then figure out a way to increase your means so that you can get out of consumer debt. Getting out of debt is, in my books, not necessarily a priority, but making more money is definitely a priority, while you keep your intentions to whittle down consumer debt.

There is no point getting out of debt when you don't know how to make more money, because as soon as you are out, you will be right back in again. You have seen this happen before. I know it's not news to you.

There are of course different categories of debt and some of these are mentioned in the section on Debt.

Your Money's Friends and Foes

The next thing you need to understand about savings, are things that eat up your money, and things that make your money grow. "Where did all the money go?" is the question that many of us ask ourselves every month just after payday. We ask this because we don't know what's eating our money up. It's as if we've put it in pockets with holes in them. You need to understand your budget as was discussed earlier.

- Bad spending habits and indiscipline may be what you need to tackle and overcome.
- Another creator of holes in your pocket is of course those high interest rates. They are the termites that gnaw at your wealth bit by bit, like my lawn that was once so promising, but has now been reduced to a dusty patch of ground.
- For those of you who are prudent stewards of your money, you need to understand how inflation nibbles at your loot over time, and outsmart it by adding inflation adjusters to your savings.
- Impatience, whose opposite will be discussed below, is another crippling factor in the construction of your financial empire.

Your money's friends

Two things, among others, that make your money grow, are compound interest and time! You can't build a house overnight. Not a strong house anyway!

An old truism about investing is this:
- Financial wealth is created over long periods of time, not day trading. If you get all your ducks in a row quickly, there is nothing that can stop you from becoming wealthy within a reasonable amount of time depending won what you do and your level of commitment.
- The second friendly element to the construction of your wealth is of course, Compound interest. Albert Einstein called compound interest the 8th wonder of the world.

Compound interest thrives on time. This is when your interest earns interest. With long term investment and compound interest, the sooner you start the better.

That old adage rings true: procrastination is the

thief of, not only time, but also wealth in this case. Hopefully by now you are ready to ask the all-important question of "how much should I save"? Well, would you like to become a millionaire?

> If you invest 67.00 bucks per month starting at age 20, invest this at 11%, and at age 65 you will have a million bucks! That's only 2.25 bucks per day! It sounds extraordinary, but it's true! You do the maths!
>
> A 25-year-old will have to invest 117.00 bucks while a 30-year-old will have to part with 203.00 bucks to make the big bucks. The longer you wait, the more you will have to fork out. At 35, you need 357.00 bucks, while at 40 you will have to give up 635.00 bucks per month. Of course, the assumption is that the interest growth rate averages 11% the whole time.

Time, Discipline and Compound interest should be your loyal friends in the construction of your future nest egg.

The above, of course, is the traditional way of making a million bucks. There are newer ways of making money and building wealth.

Well, if it seems so easy why don't we have more millionaires? Because young people don't think about savings until it's too late. Older folks forget about inflation, which will play havoc with your money if you have no inflation adjusters in your savings.

Before you rush out to the bank let me state that there are different savings criteria that you need to follow:

Funding your emergencies

You need to distinguish between Pure Emergency Fund (PEF) and Non-Emergency Fund (NEF). *Non-Emergency Fund* (NEF) is the amount after all expenses have been paid and emergency allotment has been satisfied. It is also called the reserve fund.

Pure Emergency Fund, on the other hand, is the amount set aside for emergencies such as losing your job, car problems, or a non-reimbursable medical event.

Most experts recommend at least three to six months of expenses to be set aside for the "PEF" account. This should be done before any investing of "NEF" is done.

This money may be put in a very safe investment such as a call account, money market account, a fixed deposit or a 32-day notice account.

Since it is allocated as an emergency fund, you don't want to lock it away into long term savings, but you also want to be able to have it earning reasonable interest. 32 day is fairly liquid.

If the emergency is very immediate, you could finance it with your credit card and then apply to your bank to release these funds to cover your credit card.

Many credit cards have a window in which you do not pay interest. Once this Emergency amount has been satisfied, then you should feel comfortable starting your investment program. The last thing you want to do is have to liquidate your long-term investment portfolio to meet short-term obligations that were unexpected. Avoid cancelling a long-term insurance policy to meet a short-term emergency. We call this dipping into principal to meet income needs.

This is a pretty simple concept but an important one, as we need to be good shepherds of our financial resources and not find ourselves stressed out because of some unexpected expense. Plan, not fear, for the unexpected and stay calm and at peace with whatever happens. No matter how diligently you build your financial empire, failure to purchase adequate insurance can put you in a desperate hole in a heartbeat!

SELF-ASSESSMENT

1. What is the importance of starting a pay yourself first habit?

2. List some of your money's enemies and state why they are enemies.

3. List your money's friends and state why they are considered your money's friends.

4. How will you take advantage of your money's friends?

Never depend on single income. Make investment to create a second source

Barren Buffet

CHAPTER 4

4. YOUR PERSONAL MONEY TREE

"You can only become truly accomplished at something you love… pursue the things you love doing, and then do them so well that people can't take their eyes off you."

Maya Angelou

LEARNING OUTCOMES

In this chapter you will learn:
1. How to find your own money trees
2. Personal skills inventory process
3. The importance of additional sources of income

"Money does not grow on trees" is a reality for a lot of people. But what does that mean? For the most part it means that making money is not easy. It means money is not a commodity that you could just pick off trees like you can pick summer fruit.

But what if we believed that money grows on trees? A belief that money grows on trees is equivalent to the belief that making money is easy.

In this chapter I want to talk about the money tree. I would like for you to suspend your belief that money does not grow on trees. I would like for you to consider the possibility that it does actually grow on trees. If it did, I guess your first question would be: where are the trees upon which money grows? What if I told you that you are the tree? The seeds are resident within you and the purpose of this chapter is to reveal to you your own "acres of diamonds" as Russell Conwell used to say.

Russell Conwell was a man who, in the 1930s went all over the United States telling people that they were standing on their own "acres of diamonds" if they only looked within. He tells of men who sold their lands and went too far away lands to look for diamonds, only for diamonds to be discovered from the lands they sold. He tells of men who stopped three feet from gold and sold their equipment, only for the buyer of the equipment to mine the wealth. That speech is still available today and you can find it on the Templeton university website.

The Money Tree is the thing that can bring the cash in. All you have to do is nurture it and take care of it. We all have our own money tree(s).

How do you find your own Money Tree?

Think about yourself this way: if you have a job, you are probably selling a certain number of hours (usually eight) per day to an employer who is interested in a particular skill that you have.

The next question you have to ask yourself is: is that the only skill that you have? The answer is, for the most part: of course not!

But if you are like most people, the skill that your employer is buying from you is the only skill that you are selling, and therefore it is the only skill that brings money into your personal money field.

Many of us feel like we don't even own that skill anymore because we have probably signed a non-compete clause with the employer "to never use that skill outside of the business of the employer". If that is the case, you may feel like the employer owns the money tree, the only money tree you have ever nurtured and developed.

Where then do I find another money tree? Before we think about other skills totally unrelated to your primary skill, consider your primary skill and figure out what other subsidiary skills you have learned that may or may not be related to the main skill itself.

If you are an accountant for example, consider the fact that organisational skill, which your employer is not necessarily paying for, could be employed by you in other ventures. If you are a good lawyer, the chances are your public speaking skills are good, and if you found another topic over which you are passionate, you could make money being a motivational speaker or a trainer.

To have a good start in nurturing your money tree, it is important that you start with what you know. If you want to start a business, start it in the field that you already know.

Why do businesses fail, especially start-up businesses? Loral Langemeier, author of *The Millionaire Maker* says most entrepreneurs fail because they choose to pursue entrepreneurship with new skills instead of with known skills.

People have a "dream" business in a field that they know nothing about, and instead of making money the day they open, they spend more time trying to figure out how that particular industry works. They can't be in the conversation because they don't know the language of that industry. So, they end up losing money instead of making money.

That would be like a teacher wanting to go into the hospitality industry like tourism, but because she has never operated there, she would have to spend much more time trying to learn the language of the industry instead of making money.

What do you think would be the fastest way to cash for a teacher? Should she not stay in the teaching industry? The reason she wants to get out may be because she feels she has not been making money in that industry. All she has to do now is change her revenue model. She has been receiving her money as an employee, now she can receive her money as an entrepreneur, perhaps by starting a private tutoring company; the key word being company.

That means she does not have to be the one

teaching the lessons, but she has to manage the business. How? She still has her full-time job. There are only few weekends in a month. How is she going to run a tutoring business?

Here is a better question: how many students from the university or those waiting to go to tertiary institutions can you find that would like to make extra money on the weekend?

Of course, there are plenty. So, you hire them to give lessons to junior school kids? Yes. All they need is an entrepreneur who can manage them. Someone to do the marketing and get new students enrolled; a place to operate from; someone to manage the accounting and the scheduling. That's where the experienced teacher comes in. She selects those tutors who were best in their particular subjects and hires them; then get junior school kids to sign up. That is a teacher's fastest way to cash. She could be making money within two weeks.

A musician could start a coaching team for kids wanting to start a band. A sports teacher could teach tennis lessons, etc.

You get the idea. Focus on what you know now, before breaking into a field you don't know. The keyword in business is cash flow. Figuring out the fastest way to cash could generate money for your future "dream" business.

Personal Skills Inventory

Draw up a personal skills inventory list. As we mentioned earlier, always start with what you know. Look at your current job and figure out how many skills it takes to accomplish it.

By that I don't mean how many people, I mean, how many skills, all of which are performed by you, does it take to get your job done.

What exactly do you do at your job? List all the activities regardless of what your official job description says. Don't just write Human Resources. Break it down.

- o Do you do recruitment and hiring?

- Do you headhunt?
- Do you interview?
- Do you train?
- Do you develop training material?
- Do you deal with Industrial relations issues?
- Do you counsel employees?
- Do you liaise with industry partners in any way?
- Do you deal with payroll?
- Do you do exit interviews?
- Do you deal with CVs?

All these are different skills that it takes to do your job, and if you think about it, you could specialise in any one of these and become an expert in that field. Can you see that?

Take about 90 minutes of uninterrupted time and list your entire skill set. Think about everything. What did you do when you were younger? What are some skills that you applied in previous jobs that you no longer use now? Is there a way you could build businesses around these skills?

In the next chapter, we look at how you can sell these skills and bring more money into your money field.

INCOME	EXPENSES
Tools for bringing more income o Skills o Talents o Education o Qualifications o Experience	
ASSETS	**LIABILITIES**

SELF-ASSESSMENT

1. "Money grows on trees" – explain

2. What is the process of finding your own money trees?

3. How can you break down your current skill into multiple skills?

4. Which skills remain "unemployed" in your own personal life?

5. What will you do about your own unemployed skills?

Chapter 5

5. MARKETING YOUR PERSONAL SKILLS

"It's not how much money you make, but how much money you keep, how hard it works for you, and how many generations you keep it for."

Robert Kiyosaki

LEARNING OUTCOMES

In this chapter you will learn:

1. Various entities that will be interested in your skills
2. Entities with vested interest in your particular skill set

Who Has Money to Give You?

The question of who has money to give you has several layers: First, who would be interested in your particular skill set and talents, as well as the products and services that you would offer?

Second, if they are interested, do they have money to acquire your services?

Third, do they have the authority to make a purchase decision?

Identifying your particular target market using these layers helps you not to waste time with people that are just interested but can't buy either because they have no money or no authority. Market research is simply you trying to figure out who will pay you for what you can do.

There are various categories of entities with

money, and each one of them uses a different method to acquire services. Consider the following list of entities with money:

1. Individual consumers

If your product, service, skill, or talent is geared towards individual consumers, you need to start separating those who interest, money, and authority from the rest. Understand the buying behaviour of individual consumers.

2. Businesses

Businesses generally only buy goods and services that will help them to either be more profitable or more efficient in carrying out their core business. Is there a way that you can align your skills, talents, goods, or services to fit in with the objectives of the businesses you are trying to sell to?

3. Government

Governments acquire goods and services through the tendering system. If you want to sell to government, you need to familiarize yourself with the tendering system.

Many governments are outsourcing a lot of services that do not form the core of their functions. If you can align your skills and talents with some of these you could benefit.

Another thing which is peculiar to government is that they have a lot of programs that people out there do not understand or know how to access. If you understand these services you can make it your business to help others understand and access these programs for a fee. There are always opportunities that are worth exploring.

4. **Non-government organisations (NGO's)**

   To be able to utilize your skills and talents with NGO's you have to align yourself with what they do and understand their objectives.

Each one of these entities use a different method and motives to acquire services. Depending on the area in which you would like to focus, it is important to learn what that field requires. Generally, businesses and government have the most money, and figuring out how to sell to them might be your fastest path to cash.

The only way to make lots of money from individual consumers is you must sell to a lot of them; whereas you could make one transaction to a business or a government agency and make more money than selling to individual consumers. Businesses and governments, however, take a lot of time to make decisions, so you need to be patient.

Who Has Vested Interest?

Another way to attract money is to look at your skills and consider who would succeed if you succeeded. In other words, who has vested interest in your success.

If you are a baker, then the flower companies would benefit if you succeed because you would be utilising their flower. You could therefore go and ask them to support your project. They could fund you or support you with resources or space.

Depending on your set of skills, you could go into joint ventures with other people. You should build or join what Napoleon Hill, author of *Think and Grow Rich* called The Mastermind Group.

Do not think that you can be successful on your own. Work with others. Leverage your skills. Get support. Give support to others. There are many ways to make money. Money does grow on trees if only you would plant the seeds, nurture yourself and align yourself with the right resources.

You can get into network marketing systems. You can invest on the stock market. You can make money on the Internet. You can build your own business. You can support other people's businesses through your own business. Life is a collaborative effort. Life is a joint venture. And money grows on trees!

You could approach big business that would have vested interest in your success to incubate your business. They can house you, or give you technical support.

SELF-ASSESSMENT

1. What are your own personal skills?

2. How do you identify them?

3. Who are the entities with the most money?

4. How do you know who might have vested interest in your success?

Chapter 6

6. HOME, SWEET HOME!

"No man's family can fully enjoy life unless they do have a plot of ground wherein children can play in the clean earth ..."

George Clason

> **LEARNING OUTCOME**
> In this Chapter you will learn:
> - What to consider when buying or building your Home
> - The buyer's checklist

We all have dreams of prosperity. We would like to live in a dream house in a plush neighbourhood, driving our dream car and having our dream family, and live happily ever after! Does the saying, "Rome was not built in a day" ring a bell? How loud is the bell, you ask? If you go and ask most of the people that are currently living in their "dream" house, driving their dream car, they will tell you their previous addresses were in places they were not eager to have visitors in, and they will show you pictures of their first cars, or not, and you won't believe it.

Unless one is born into wealth or into royalty, or wins the lottery, or inherits some riches from some rich relative, most of us have to sweat it out to make it.

How do you buy or build your dream house? It's pretty much the same way that you get to your dream car. You start with a small affordable car that will get you from 'A' to 'Z'. After a few years of working, you don't just want to go from 'A' to 'Z', you want to get there 'in style'. Now you trade in your old car or sell it so that now you have a deposit for a car that will get you there in style. After a few more years, you don't just want to get there in style, you want to make a statement and also get there in comfort or Luxury. Now you sell your 'style' car so that you can get your luxury car.

How long between your 'A to Z' car and your luxury car? Not a few months! In most cases, it takes years.

Buying a home can follow a similar pattern. But many of us like short cuts, we want that posh address now, so we pay exorbitant rentals to keep up appearances, while the reality is that we are bleeding our finances to the ground. Let us consider a method you could use to acquire your dream house.

Start Early

This, however, is not for the impatient. In your

younger years after you've been working for a few years and you want to acquire a home loan, you go to the bank and the bank wants 20% down as a deposit before they can lend you the money.

Banks normally calculate 30% of your monthly income as your repayment, and they work out how much they should lend you.

If you have other loans, some banks will deduct those payments out of this 30% and work out your loan amount based on what you can pay.

You find it very difficult to raise 20% of your dream house.

In addition to this, you need to have money for transfer fees and all other initial costs.

The task seems impossible. So, you get discouraged and do nothing other than complain about how impossible banks are. Big mistake! What you should do is, go back to the bank and find out how much they will lend you, and take whatever they are willing to let you borrow. If you have a subsidy scheme from your employer, this will definitely help. With that amount go and buy the house that you can afford. Granted, that's not your dream house, but, congratulations! You are a homeowner.

Before that step however, make sure you consult your estate agent. They will tell you a whole lot more about the intricacies of buying a home than I can in this short chapter.

They will tell you about transfer fees, lawyers' fees, bond fees, and maybe their fees. Don't despair; it's how it works.

Another big question is: To build or to buy? Building may not be as cheap as you've been made to believe. Check with your real estate agent.

The buyer's Checklist

As is often said in real estate circles: Location, location, and location is the key!

When buying a home, your location is the most important element. This is a very important investment and you must guard it carefully, especially if you are going to sell it so that you can buy a better home.

Get your checklist out and examine your potential new home.

- Check for cracks in the walls, both inside and outside.
- Smell for damp and feel plastered walls for moisture.
- Be wary of new paint or wallpaper - this could be hiding cracks or damp.
- Check for woodworm and rot if the property has wooden window frames, doors and floors.
- Inspect bathrooms to see if they are well ventilated, and check if the taps work and the toilets flush properly. You wouldn't want a blocked toilet after you move in now would you?
- Any missing roof tiles? – Missing tiles could lead to leaking and other water damage.
- Check for large trees near the building as their roots could damage the foundations.

- Check the garden to see if you will need to fell any trees.
  - Are there boundary walls?
  - If not, and you have pets, it might be advisable to erect them.
  - If there are electric fences, gates and garage doors, check if they are in working order and whether they need a service.

Ask the seller as many questions as you possibly can.
  - Find out why he is moving.
  - Ask about crime in the area – or phone the local police station for crime statistics. Now, are you happy?

Next, pay that house off as quickly as you know how.

Depending on prevailing interest rates, by adding an additional two to five hundred bucks to your monthly bond, you will cut down not just interest, but the repayment period. In as quick as seven to ten years, your house could be paid off.

After you pay it off or you have taken a huge

chunk of the bond off, you may now consider selling.

Since this is not your dream home yet, you can either turn it into your dream home through extensions, and improvement if there is room for that, or you can sell.

But I'm sure you've learnt a lot about homeownership. Now get ready for the big leagues.

Since property values tend to appreciate over time, even though not all the time, especially if it's in the right location, the value of that house in seven to ten years may be a considerable amount.

Now you can approach the bank and ask them to lend you money for your dream house!

You have more than enough money as deposit, and you can pay off the transaction costs! Now you are on your way to living happily ever after. If that still does not give you your dream house, repeat the above process, or work on expanding your house to suit your style. If you start in your late twenties or early thirties, by the time you are in your fifties, you will be in your fully paid dream house.

If it is that simple, why don't more people own houses? Well, probably because of the short cut and the quick fix mentality that we are so accustomed to. What you don't know about money will hurt you!

Real Estate investing has a lot of issues that you should understand. Commit yourself to learning and growth.

SELF-ASSESSMENT

1. What is the importance of starting early when you want to buy or build a home?

2. Why is it important to have a deposit when you borrow money for a home?

3. What are some things that are important on the buyer's checklist?

Chapter 7

7. INFORMATION – THE PAPER TRAIL

"You must gain control over your money or the lack of it will forever control you."

Dave Ramsey

LEARNING OUTCOMES

In this chapter you will learn:
- Steps of Information Gathering
- Classification of Information

The interesting thing about money is that, although largely invisible, it hardly goes anywhere without leaving a paper trail. In this chapter, we will follow the paper trail. The purpose of this chapter is to help you determine where you are in your money game.

Unless you know where you are, and you fully understand how money has been flowing on your money field, can't determining exactly where you want to go and how you are going to change the flow of your money to allow you to go there.

Many people are quick to set financial goals without knowing exactly where they are, but they wonder why they are not getting there. The job of determining your position on the money field may be tedious, but unless you do it, you might as well not continue with the course. Many of us just know that 'we're in trouble'. Or that money is going out faster than is coming in and we can't figure out why. We are living from emergency to emergency, and therefore, our lives are an emergency.

Gathering information and understanding that information will go a long way in helping you understand what is going on in your financial field.

There are FOUR basic things we will have to do in this chapter. If you are serious about taking control of your money, you cannot skip this step. Without this step there is no course. For some people the work might be less than what is suggested here because they've already been running some system.

But for those who have never started before, please be patient with yourself and allow yourself to do this very important step. Here are the FOUR basic steps you will have to follow, and we will explain each of them herein.

1. INFORMATION GATHERING
2. CLASSIFICATION OF INFORMATION
3. CHOOSING AN ACCOUNTING PERIOD
4. PHYSICAL ARRANGEMENT OF INFORMATION

Please note that even if you intend to use a

computer software program, you still have to take the above steps.

Information Gathering:

Let's start with available information and then we will move on to seek missing data.

Where is my money coming from and where is it going?

A: If you are employed, you probably have a *Pay Slip.*

What information can you find on your pay slip?
- Your gross earning
- Your income tax payment
- Your medical aid information
- Your pension fund contribution
- Any other deductions that come directly from your employer like loans, life insurance, etc.
- Your net take-home pay

While the purpose of your pay slip is to answer the question, where is my money coming from, you will also find thereon information about where some of your money is going.

Your BANK STATEMENT is another source of information. What information can you find on your bank statement?

- Your income that gets paid by your employer directly into your bank account, i.e. your take home pay that remains after employer-based deductions.
- Any other deposits that you make into your account – it would be a good idea to determine the source of these deposits by keeping your deposit slips. You will also find on the bank statement information about your direct debits or your bank stop orders.
- Another piece of information that you will certainly find on your statement is bank charges or interests earned or charged.
- If this account is a Cheque account, you can trace all payments through the cheques that have been written by doing a process of *bank reconciliation*.

- If this account has a debit card that you use to make purchases, then you will have to do some work to determine what the expenses charged were for. (This may be slightly difficult if you are a kind of person who does not keep receipts.) The name of the store and the amount of the purchases will appear on your statement and perhaps you can trace what it was you were buying from that store.
- If you use your card at an ATM (Automated Teller Machine) to withdraw money, then the trick is figuring out what you did with the cash that was withdrawn
- You may find here also information about returned deposits (or bounced cheques) debited back or charged back

OTHER INFORMATION TOOLS:

If information is neither on your pay advice slip or your bank statement, and you are a kind of person who uses a lot of cash, then your best bet to gather this other information is to keep receipts every time you spend money.

If the receipt does not say what you were buying, then it will help you to note on the receipt what it is you were buying.

This information will help you when you are classifying your transactions for analysis.

Classification of Information

The best way to work with information is to classify it in a way that is meaningful to you. You classify information by creating *categories*. Categories help you to handle the amount of information you create in an organised manner. Second, it will help you to make decisions on certain categories by tracking them.

You might, for example, notice that your "eating out" expenses could be controlled more, or your phone bill can be curbed, etc.

Below is a list of possible categories. You don't have to use them all, and you can create your own that are more meaningful to you. All you have to do is avoid over generalising, or being overly specific.

Rent/Mortgage

Utilities: - Water, Electricity, Gas

Groceries

Auto: Fuel, Service, Insurance

Telephone: - Cellular phone, Home Telephone Line, Other Line (e.g. Fax/Internet)

Clothing

Give-away-money (gifts, tithe, charity)

Emergency fund

Insurance

Savings

TV – satellite/licence

School fees/Childcare

Laundry

Personal care (hair, etc)

Entertainment

Hobbies (e.g. books, CD's)

Personal Development (Further education, special subjects, special books, etc)

Household Furniture/appliances

Household helper (Maid/ gardener/ babysitter/ personal assistant, etc)

SELF-ASSESSMENT

1. What is the paper-trail?

2. On which documents will you find your important information?

3. How should you go about gathering information?

4. Why is it important to classify information?

Chapter 8

8. PHYSICAL ARRANGEMENT OF INFORMATION

"Empty pockets never held anyone back. Only empty heads and empty hearts can do that."
Norman Vincent Peale

LEARNING OUTCOMES
- Choosing an accounting period
- Physical Arrangement of Information
- How to determine where your money is coming from and where it is going

The next thing you will have to do with your information is physically arrange it in such a way that you can easily access it. It does you no good even if you keep receipts of everything if at the end of your chosen *accounting period*, you can't find it or it takes you as long to find it.

You have to designate a physical place in your home where your financial data is stored. What is the purpose of keeping physical information? There are a number of reasons why you might want to keep this data:

- First and foremost, the presence of physical data helps you keep accurate records, instead of guessing what you think you paid. In case of a dispute that you paid something, you can produce a receipt
- Many people miss out on tax deductible expenses because they can't prove that they did pay simply because they lost the receipt

There are a number of tools you can utilise to

physically store your data.

A filing Cabinet

An Arch-lever file

A filing box

A place in your home or office

Now that you have a designated place to store your information, it is not enough to just throw it in that drawer or cabinet. You need to create *physical categories.*

You have created classification categories, now you need to decide how your information will be arranged. It can be arranged in one of two ways:

- Per Accounting Period
- Per Category

Storing data by Accounting period means you file one month's information separately, and then you just arrange it by dates.

If you are using *accounting software*, you will just record your transactions as per the dates as they occur, and the software will sort them out by categories, and you will still be able to figure out how much you are spending on each category.

If you keep your information by *category*, it means of course that it does not matter whether this phone bill was for three months ago or for this month, they all go into the same place, but you will still have to arrange them by *dates* so that you can find them easily when you are looking for them.

If you use category filing, make sure that you do not create a category for each receipt, or you might run out of storage space. That is why creating your classification categories, is important.

You will also notice that some bills like school fees, for example, don't appear every month if you pay your school fees per term instead of monthly, so you might have that space having only four receipts per year.

You therefore might want to lump smaller categories together for the sake of filing space. A category like *utilities* could include all utilities like water, electricity, telephone, and gas.

If you use *period* classification, you will only

need 12 files for the year, or just one Arch-Lever file for the year, instead of 15 or 20 little files depending on the number of categories you create.

So, whether you buy a large file box, or clear out a drawer in your bedroom, or install a new program on your computer, the same principle applies: You can only stay organized if there's a physical place for all the paper and information you need to track throughout the year. No matter the system, create your categories in advance. Then whenever you have an important piece of information to save, it will already have a home. These are some of the key file/folder categories for your project:

Expenses: This cabinet drawer/box/file holds all your bills from utilities to medical bills to taxes.

You can further subcategorise your expenses folder so that you can track the telephone bills, utilities, groceries, petrol and travel, or rental, etc.

Your next category is Banking. This folder will help you keep monthly statements, cancelled cheques and deposit receipts. At the end of the month when you do your bank reconciliation, all the information will already be in one place. Next is your Investments folder. Your insurance policies and any other investments documents go into this folder. This will also help you to monitor how you are doing as an investor.

Choosing an Accounting Period

This should be relatively easy to do. All you do in this step is decide whether you will file your information weekly, fortnightly, monthly, bimonthly or quarterly.

If you are a beginner, I will avoid a longer period and stick to an average period such as a MONTHLY period. In fact, in the beginning, to gain momentum, it might help you to file weekly, just until you pick up momentum and you are serious about this process.

Then you can move off to monthly and keep it there. Your accounting period can coincide with your bank statement period so that you can do your bank reconciliation easily.

Some bank statements start say on the 7th to the 6th and most people like working from the 1st to the 30th. Don't get thrown off if your statement is like that.

The bank normally starts on the day that you opened your account and will choose that as your statement period.

It is much easier to keep the same date or you could ask them to change your statement period to start at the start of the month to the end of the month. What is the importance of an accounting period?

An accounting period allows you to compare, say last month with the month before. An accounting period provides a yardstick against which you can measure your progress.

Information-Gathering Sheet

Money Goals and Money Management Tools

You may benefit from a use of an information-gathering sheet. As we said, you can use a weekly information sheet, or a monthly sheet. This is a sheet with days of the week on the left, and categories at the top, and each time you spend money in a particular category, you record it there. Here's an example.

	Transport	Food	Phone	Other
Monday				
Tuesday				
Wednesday				
Thursday				
Friday				
Saturday				
Sunday				

You may of course design your own sheet that suits your needs better. You may also have a monthly sheet with dates, 1 to 31 on the left, and categories at the top. The trick will be not to forget to record your financial activities, or to leave it until you forget what the receipt was for.

SELF-ASSESSMENT

1. What is an accounting period?

2. What tools can you use to physically store data?

3. What is the purpose of keeping physical information?

4. Which categories are relevant to you?

5. What is the use of having an information gathering sheet?

Chapter 9

9. CREATING RECORDS

"Wealth is the ability to fully experience life."

Henry David Thoreau

> **LEARNING OUTCOMES:**
> In this chapter you will learn:
> - Recording of Information
> - Income and Expense Statement
> - Cash flow Statement
> - Balance Statement

This chapter could be the most practical of all of them since it involves the recording of all the information that you have gathered in a significant manner. Taking this step is as important as the steps you have taken in the previous chapter. However, without this step, all you have done in the previous chapter will be in vain.

If you are utilising an accounting software, this will be easy since all you have to do now is enter the data according to the decision you have made.

After this, with most computer software packages, all you have to do is ask it questions and it will whip up for you in a matter of seconds the kinds of reports that you require. Some packages may even offer you some analysis to help you understand the figures.

You will do well to remember that these packages cannot make up your mind for you, so you still have to make decisions and interpret the information according to what your goals are. Now that you have your information at hand, we can start talking about creating your financial baseline.

Bank Reconciliation Statement

One of the processes that will help you to have correct information is the process of Cheque Book Balancing or Bank Reconciliation Statement.

The purpose of reconciling your records with those of the bank as reflected on your bank statement, is to make sure that you and the bank are in agreement about the amount of money that you really have.

It is possible that you would think you have a certain amount of money in your bank account, meanwhile the bank has increased their bank charges, and you write a cheque that will bounce back to you. Or a cheque deposit that you have made has been bounced or returned to the drawer for one reason or another.

Or your bank statement is reflecting a balance bigger than what you thought you had, because a cheque that you wrote has not yet been presented to the bank for clearing.

Cheque Book Balancing

The process of bank reconciliation really starts with you balancing your own cheque book.

Depending which bank you are with, each cheque book has a Transaction form or a cheque stub upon which you should keep a record of each transaction that you make. This form allows you to record each withdrawal or deposit, keeping a 'running balance' at all times.

If you balance your cheque book every time you use your cheque book, you will almost always know approximately how much money you have in your bank account.

If you have a debit card attached to the account, you will have to remember to come and update your cheque book after each charge, so that you are always up to date with your account.

Now that you have kept your records straight, you can now compare your records with the records of the bank, to make sure that there is agreement.

This is the process of bank reconciliation. You basically compare your records with those of the bank, noting the differences and adjusting until you are in agreement.

Other Essential Financial Records

The purpose of creating Financial Records is to figure out where you are at in the financial game. To simplify this process, your records may contain basic lists, to begin with. You first list is of course a list of all your sources of income

Your next list is a list of all your usual expenses. Then comes the dreaded list of debts – all your debts. The next list is a list of all your assets. With these lists you will be creating three statements:

Section A: Income And Expense

Statement

Your <u>Income and Expense Statement</u>, otherwise referred to as you Income Statement = serves to compare your income with your expenses.

Expenses do not only refer to cash expensed, but expenses include such things as your accounts like your telephone account, whether you paid it that month or not. When the bill arrives, it is an expense because you have already consumed (whatever it is the telephone company sells, i.e., talk time). Likewise, when your water bill arrives, whether you have paid it or not, it is an expense because you have already consumed the water.

Section B: Statement of Cash Flow

You <u>Statement of Cash Flow</u> will monitor the flow of your cash. This statement focuses only on hard cash. You don't include money someone else owes you if you have not yet received it, and you only record cash as it goes out. This is different to your income statement because some cash will go to other items that are not classified as 'expenses', such as savings, etc.

Section C: Balance Sheet

Then you will create your Balance Sheet. This represents your net-worth. This statement is not as fluid as the first two. It is sort of like a picture over a certain period of time, usually a year or more.

It is a list of all your assets up to that particular time, as well as all the liabilities pitied against such assets.

For example, while you might list your house as an asset, the mortgage on the house is the liability pitied against the asset.

The difference between the value of the house and the amount of the mortgage still owed, represents the real value of the house to you.

That is, if you sold your house today at that value, you will have to settle the mortgage first, and what remains could be said to be your real asset.

From all these statements, you will be able to get your Net Worth.

What is your growth strategy going forward?

Income Strategy	Expense Strategy
Asset growth Strategy	Debt Strategy

SELF-ASSESSMENT

1. Give reasons why it is important to balance your statement or cheque book

2. List and highlight the differences by defining the three types of financial statements

3. What is a bank reconciliation statement and why is it important?

4. How does the cash flow statement differ from the income statement?

Chapter 10

10. A JOURNEY OF DISCOVERY

Warning: This chapter and the next, if taken seriously, could be the most intense chapters of the entire book, and they may prove to be very important. This chapter will ask very practical and personal questions. If you engage this process, you will come out on the other side a changed person.

The purpose of this chapter is to help you appreciate where you are situated psychologically with regard to your finances. Give yourself a chance to answer the following questions honestly. Some of them may seem mundane and shallow, until you consider the deeper meaning within each question, and the ripple effect that the answer could have on your finances.

Allow yourself to *think* about this subject *deeply*. Until your mind is engaged and your emotions stirred, you will take the practical portions of this programme lightly and it will not be of use to you. So, I urge you to engage your mind and to allow yourself to feel!

Note that many of our habits pertaining to money are second nature. We don't have to think about these actions any more. They happen automatically. The purpose of this programme is to CHALLENGE your second nature, and perhaps to change it, especially if it is not working for you.

The best way to change your habits is to challenge them. You challenge them by holding them up to the light of scrutiny and logic. When you stop and consider some of the things you have done without really thinking about them, do they make sense? Are they serving you? Are your actions beneficial to you?

As the saying goes, when the student is ready, the teacher will appear. The student is the one who asks questions. So, the outline of this programme is from a student's point of view so it is a question- based outline. This chapter seeks to answer the following basic questions:

A. Income: Where is my money coming from?

B. Expenses: Where is my money going?

C. Balance Sheet: What is my money doing for me? Or, what is my net worth?

SECTION A: INCOME

Income: Where is my money coming from? What is the source of my income? List all your regular sources of income and their frequency:

- Employment,

- Business,
- Investments
- loans (overdraft/credit cards),
- Gifts and grants, etc.

Many people are on a revolving credit system. For example, if you earn 5'000.00, you have a revolving credit of 3'000.00, you therefore THINK you live a lifestyle worth 8'000.00, when, in reality, you are actually still living on 5'000.00. At the end of every month, your account is at negative -3'000.00. Your salary comes in, fills up the hole and you have a positive balance of 2'000.00, and you spend it, plus the 3'000.00-revolving credit. The difference is of course that the -3'000.00 is borrowed money for consumption and it always comes at a cost.

How does my money get to me?
Consider the path your money is following before it reaches you, because along some paths are many predators.

Your money could come to you via a bank account; or a cheque in your hand for you to cash; or an e-wallet for you to go get at the ATM; or cash, etc.

Who takes my money before I get it? Asked another way; who has access to my money before it reaches me?

Are there predators on your money's path? Not everyone who has access to your money before you do is a predator. Some are good beneficiaries like your retirement contribution, because that's still money belonging to you. But some are true predators and once they have your money, you will never see it again.

Even if you have cash in your hand, consider that when you deposit it in an account, there will be a predator called, "cash deposit fee". If you withdraw money, there is the "withdrawal fee" predator. Don't forget about these little seemingly invisible guys when you list the beneficiaries and the predators on your money's path. Look at your pay slip and you will soon spot them.

Why is it coming from there?

There are various reasons why your money could be coming from where it comes from. Employment, sales of goods and services, allowance, gifts, loans, etc.

How steady is the source of my income?

This question has a bearing on your future planning. Is this source dependable? Is it sustainable? If some of your income is from people who owe you, you need to consider: Have they forgotten to pay you? Do they need a reminder? Are they genuinely unable to pay you and ou need to consider writing off the debt and stop hoping and expecting? People often make promises to others based on what someone else has promised to pay them. If this source is unreliable, you could be creating problems for yourself.

Where else could it come from?

This question allows you to start thinking of alternative sources of income. Are there opportunities out there that you could start pursuing? These could include selling stuff you no longer need, getting a new job, starting a side business, joining a network marketing organisation that resonates with you, etc.

What processes and procedures have I set in place to ensure that my money continues to come from where it is coming?

This is a very important question to consider because it goes to the core of your daily routines. This helps you to examine your <u>income- producing activities</u>. Examine the use of your resources such as time. If you have a job and you leave home at 7am and you are back at 7pm. If you are running a business, how much time do you spend on marketing, or creating new products, or working <u>on</u> your business instead of just working <u>in</u> your business?

What new processes and procedures can I introduce to have my money coming from somewhere else, or where

I would rather it came from? (that is, from something that I really enjoy).

In other words, is my current system my fastest way to generate cash, or is there another option?

Now that you have considered what you are currently doing, you need to consider what you can do to improve your processes. The purpose of this programme is to help you along that path. Here you list your desires, and later in the book your possibilities should become clearer.

OBSERVATIONS

In this section, you may have, for the first time in your life, thought about the sources of your income in detail. This exercise will go a long way towards ensuring that you get involved in this process of understanding your finances.

Notes on this Section:

SECTION B: EXPENSES

Expenses: Where is my money going? What is my money doing?

This may sound like a strange question to ask of your money, but there are basic things that your money is doing for you, like: My money keeps me out of trouble with my creditors every month. In other words, without it, I'd be in serious trouble. Or, my money keeps me in survival mode, or my money feeds me, or it educates me, or it pays for my shelter, or it keeps me in luxury and enjoying life, or it grows my net worth. This question gets you to start understanding how you employ your money, and later on you will start questioning or improving upon how your money is employed.

Where is my money going?

Again, another seemingly simple question, but, as you write down where your money goes every month, you might consider changing its direction. You don't write the amounts or the justifications, just the people and places where your money goes, such as landlords, filling stations, grocery stores, bars, other people, etc.

Don't write "rent," or "entertainment," that is the justification. Write the name of your landlord or the owner of the bar, etc. Putting down the names of the people you're paying your money to is going to produce a different emotion than you will feel when noting the justification. If, instead of rent you write Joe Smith, you might start wondering how much of his mortgage you have paid. That might be just the information that is necessary to wake you up.

How long has it been going there?

One of the things that can strongly motivate you to buy a house, is if you consider how long you've been paying landlords! Before I bought my own house, I made a compilation of the amounts and landlords I had paid over the previous three years. Three years was enough to convince me. Link the answers to this question with those in the previous question.

How does it go there?

Again, considering the path followed by your money will help you determine if that path is safe or if it has predators along the way. You know that when you write a cheque, there is often a "cheque clearing fee". If you do a stop order, there is a "transaction fee". If you swipe a debit card, it's often a free transaction, but not always.

An over-the-counter withdrawal may have a charge, while an ATM withdrawal may have a smaller or no charge. These charges are often there to let you know which method your bank prefers. By not charging you for an ATM withdrawal, they are hoping you can go there instead of coming into the bank to be attended to by a person they have to employ and pay, which increases their running costs.

Why is it going there?

This question requires you to ponder the motives behind your actions. Is your money going there to meet a real need that exists or to satisfy an ego drive? This is where you can list your justifications such as rental or entertainment.

Should it be going where it is going?

This question requires you to ponder your values. As in all other questions, there is no right or wrong answer, just observations. You may approach this by saying, given what you say you want in life, is this the best use of your resources? In other words, **does this expense help me to reach my desired goals or is it holding me back?** Is it serving me to have my money going where it is going?

Would I rather it went somewhere else? If so, why?

This question calls for a re-examination of your purpose and whether your financial processes support your purpose. Of course, if you are paying for debt of consumables that are no longer around, you would probably prefer that your money went somewhere else. But this question might get you thinking in terms of the processes that led to your money going where it is currently going.

What habits and behaviours are propelling my money in the direction it is going?

A habit is a behaviour that you have performed so many times that it has become automatic. There are debt habits, impulsive buying habits, competitive habits, etc. This question begins to tap into the root of the issue. The psychology of money is a subject of another book, but this gives you an idea of what it entails. Can you identify your habits?

What beliefs do I adhere to that drive my financial behaviour in this direction?

At the core of every action that we take is a belief, and that belief, when strongly held, creates behaviours that eventually become regarded as "common sense". When something is "common sense", it means it has become second nature. One of the core purposes of this programme is to challenge such beliefs that propel or drive certain behaviours.

A belief that says, "of course I can't afford this without taking a loan", has "obviously" ruled out alternatives such as: sell something I don't currently need to raise the cash for this; or wait until I save enough money; or, create another way of making extra cash, etc.

What processes and procedures have I set in place to have my money going where it is currently going?

Processes and procedures are everything. Everything in life is systematic. Everything follows a process. If you are paying for consumer debt, you might want to consider where that process began, what point it has reached, and when it will end. Your process here might be a signed stop order or a debit order, or it may be a monthly visit to the bank to stand in a long queue for many hours just to give money to your landlord, or to pay the debt to your clothing store for clothes that you don't wear anymore; or to pay your credit card for food you consumed three months ago.

What new processes and procedures would I have to set in place for my money to change direction and go where I would rather it went?

The new processes might include a debt-repayment programme, or a budget, or a savings programme, etc. It is important to understand the power of processes and procedures. Once a process is in place, we often forget about it, but if it is a process that gets money out of my pocket, then I should know whether it is empowering me or disempowering me.

There are processes like direct deductions

from your salary for insurance policies, that may not be serving their purposes any longer. Perhaps there was a family funeral cover you took, but one of the family members has since passed on, yet you have not adjusted that process. Or you have married and had a baby and they are not covered on your old policy.

All of our systems are made up of processes. All facets of life run on systems. Even poverty is a system. It is a set of arranged processes that would have to change if wealth were to come into play. Your current systems many not be set up to receive wealth. Wealth does not come where there is confusion, but where there is clarity. Get it clear in your mind what your new systems are and how they will function.

YOUR NOTES ON THIS CHAPTER:

Chapter 11

11. MY NET WORTH – WHAT HAS MY MONEY DONE FOR ME?

The Balance Sheet is the measure of your net worth. In financial or numeric terms, if you add up all your assets and then subtract all your liabilities, that is your net worth. This tells the story of what you've been up to all your life. It presents a static photo, summarising your state at this present moment. So, if we were to freeze everything right now and examine your financial affairs, what would we see?

The following questions are designed to illustrate your current status, if nothing else were to happen. It is very important in this state to not only focus on the numeric figures represented by your statements. The most valuable assets of each individual can often not be represented on the traditional balance sheet.

What has my money done for me?
This question seeks to summarise the accomplishments that you have achieved with your money. There are more detailed questions below. The answer to this question may necessitate a quick addition of all your assets, minus all your liabilities, to see whether the answer is pleasing to you or not. Do not let the answer discourage you, but let it spur you on to work on your finances. This figure might be negative or positive, but either way, it does not matter. What is important at this stage is that you are taking charge of your

finances.

What tangible things has my money done for me?

This question seeks to enumerate the tangible things that your money has done for you thus far. It is a simple straight forward list of all your assets with their numeric values.

What intangible things has my money done for me?

It would be a mistake to assume that the only things valuable are things that are tangible. You may feel that there are other assets that you have bought with your money, but these are intangible. These may include skills you have learned and paid for, even in "sweat equity".

If you have taken a course to acquire some new skill, all you might have to point to is perhaps a certificate, or not, but the value of that skill will go on to earn you success. List such intangible assets here.

In accounting terms, they may not carry value on a traditional Balance Sheet, but you know that they have improved your life, and so it is important that you recognise them. If the previous list of tangible things has discouraged you, perhaps all is not lost. This is an area you can look at and get the boost in energy that you need to propel you forward.

Your internal skills may yet be your most valued assets. They may not have financial value attached to them, but they are invaluable to your progress. (I know for me my typing skill, which I learned at high school, has saved me lots of time and money since I did not have to pay anyone to type my school projects or my other writing projects. I don't have to write things down in pen first, have them typed by someone, brought back to me for editing, and then rewrite them.) Of course, since I can still type over 100 words per minute, it saves me plenty of time.

Are my assets increasing in value or are they depreciating?

This question seeks to examine the type of assets that you have purchased. You might say: Well, all assets depreciate in value with the exception of real estate. However, if a business is something that you have purchased with your money, and it is getting better and better, then you have an asset that is increasing in value. If you purchased a skill with your money, you might want to ask yourself whether that skill is just a certificate hanging on the wall while you have forgotten everything you have learned, or whether that skill is increasing in value since it is now able to bring you more money than it did initially.

What are my liabilities?

You will not know what your net worth is until you know how much of the money in your possession is actually not yours, or how indebted you are to other people. This is a simple listing of all your debt.

What am I doing with other people's money?

Part of considering what your money is doing for you is to consider what you are doing with other people's money. Too often we take out loans but we can't really say what we have done with other people's money, and when they want it back, we find the repayment stressful. When you borrow money, do you borrow to help yourself grow or you just borrow for consumption? Now consider the question again: **What have you been doing with other people's money?**

Am I getting better off or am I worse off?
This question seeks to establish another level of analysis of your assets. Are the so-called assets actually dragging more and more money out of your pocket, or are they putting money in your pocket? Too often we buy things that we call assets, say a second-hand car, and for them to function, we need to keep adding more and more money into it just to hold on to it. Sometimes you are just better off letting go and saving your money, instead of bleeding yourself into the ground with something that will never get better.

Am I set up to grow or to shrink?

This question seeks to help you figure out whether, considering the way you are going, are you set up to grow, albeit slowly, or are you, slowly but surely, sinking? What is your set up? Will you get promotion at work because of your newly acquired skill, or if you just sit there, will you be retrenched or fired? Is this company growing or sinking? If you are in business, what is your set up? Are you set up to grow or will you be run over? Have you invested in new products or new markets?

Am I happy with my net worth?

Most people are not happy with their net worth. You may not be happy with your net worth and therefore seek to improve it. You may, however, seek to determine what will make you happy at this stage of your life. This means you set a target that you believe you will be happy with when you achieve it. (It does not mean that when you get there you will not have a desire for more, but right now, that is what you should focus on.) Say, **in the next 12 months, what improvements do you want to see in terms of your net worth?**

What can I do now?

This speaks of your opportunity to set up a new game plan. Do I go and acquire a new skill? Do I utilise the skill that I now have but have not yet fully utilised? Do I sell some of the assets that are draining money out of my pocket? Do I acquire new assets that will put money in my pocket? Do I go out and seek more advice? Do I set up a vigorous sales campaign in my business?

What new processes and procedures would I have to set up to have my money doing for me what I would rather it did for me?

Nothing happens without processes and procedures in place. Wishful thinking does not get anything done. Your current life follows processes that you have set in place. Watch yourself, you will see that you are following processes and procedures, most of them subconsciously. What you have to do right now is determine whether those processes and procedures are serving you or not. Watch your income-producing patterns and your spending patterns. You may decide to commit to a debt-elimination plan so that you can use the funds currently funding your debt to buy real assets or a business or shares in a business.

SUMMARY

The questions asked above will help to reveal a lot about the paths that your money is following. An honest answer to each of the questions will help to make this journey an easy one, albeit, not necessarily an easy one from an emotional standpoint. An honest answer to some of the questions might get you emotionally involved, but it would be helpful to get back to your senses quickly without getting overwhelmed, so let's get to work. With a positive attitude, everything is possible.

ACKNOWLEDGEMENTS

The recreation of this book series was as a result of the revision of *Functional Mastery Over My Finances*. We created a course that got accredited by Botswana Qualifications Authority (BQA). We needed a more relevant "text book" that could accompany the course.

Once I had ploughed through the material, my colleague and fellow personal finance educator Poloko Mongatane was a great help in not only pushing for the accreditation of the course, but getting her hands dirty and helping to create some of the assessment questions at the end of some of the chapters, as well as doing some editing.

All this was supposed to be one big book. In fact, the three-in-one paperback version remains one book divided into three parts. The book series idea however came in a bit to reduce the book to chewable chunks instead of one big bite.

Great thanks to all the people who have given feedback since the publication of the first book in 2008. Many thanks also to all the workshop participants who brought in new perspectives on some of the concepts and for helping to improve them.

Many thanks to my staff at Moedi Financial Training for their constant support. Oteng "Owty" Orakanye, many of the workshops that have happened to improve this material would not have happened without you.

My gratitude goes to my family always for their unending support.

Thank you

Nelson Letshwene

THANK YOU

If you enjoyed reading this book, please feel free to leave me a review. Reviews help other readers to know the relevance of the book for them and they help authors like me to improve on our work for the benefit of our readers.

Nelson Letshwene

About the Author

Nelson Letshwene is a Financial Planner and author of several books including *Your Longing Is Your Calling*; *The Money Field* Series, and the Faith and Prayer series of books.

He holds a bachelor's degree in Business Economics from the University of the Witwatersrand (Johannesburg), a post graduate business degree from The University of South Africa (Pretoria), and a post graduate diploma in Financial Planning from Milpark Education (Cape Town)

You can connect with him on social media:

Facebook: Money Skills with Nelson Letshwene

You Tube: Money Skills with Nelson Letshwene

or

https://www.youtube.com/channel/UCQoXuEwcNDyqf1_EW70w3gA

Twitter: @NelsonLetshwene

BIBLIOGRAPHY

1. Abraham Jay, 1995, 2002, 9 Pillars to business growth, Torrance, CA, Abraham Publishing group, Inc.
2. Berger Rob, Top 100 Money Quotes of all time, www.forbes.com
3. Cameron, B. 2003. Getting Started: Money Matters for Under 25s. Cape Town: Zebra Press
4. Cameron, B. 2003. Massive fraud in funeral assurance industry exposed. Personal Finance: 1, August 9.
5. Cameron, B. 2003. Steep rise in lapsed policies. Personal Finance:1. September 27.
6. Clark, J.B. 1990. Marketing Today – Successes, Failures, and Turnarounds, 2nd eds. New Jersey: Prentice-Hall Inc.
7. Clason George S, 1926, The Richest Man in Babylon, Penguin books
8. Griffin, G. Edward, 1994, The Creature from Jekyll Island, American Media
9. Hill, Napolean, 1937, Think and Grow Rich, Fawcett books, New York
10. Johnson, S. Et al. 1999. Saving Faith. Boston: DPI
11. Kiyosaki, R.T and Lechter, S.L 1997. Rich Dad Poor Dad, - what the rich teach their kids about money that

the poor and middle class do not. New York, Warner Books Inc.
12. Kiyosaki, R.T and Lechter, S.L 1999. Cashflow Quadrant, New York, Warner Books Inc
13. Kiyosaki, R.T and Lechter, S.L 2000. Rich Dad's Guide to becoming rich, without cutting up your credit cards. New York. Warner Audio Books.
14. Kiyosaki, R.T and Lechter, S.L 2000. Rich Dad's Guide to Investing. New York. Warner Books.
15. Kiyosaki, R.T and Lechter, S.L 2001-2005, The Business School, 2nd ed, Momentum Media.
16. Kiyosaki, R.T and Lechter, S.L 2008, Increase Your Financial IQ, New York, Business Plus
17. Landsburg, Steven, E, 1993, The Armchair Economist, Simon & Schuster, London
18. Langemeier, Loral, 2005, The Millionaire Maker, McGraw-Hill
19. Langemeier, Loral, 2007, The Millionaire Maker's Guide to creating a Cash Machine for life, McGraw-Hill
20. Langemeier, Loral, 2009, Put More Cash in your Pocket: Turn what you know into dough, Harper Paperbacks
21. Lechter, M, Other People's Money, Warner Books, New York
22. Letshwene, R.N, 2008, Functional Mastery Over My Finances, Reach Publishers
23. Letshwene, R.N. 2004, UNISA, Personal Financial Management in Botswana
24. Letshwene, R.N. 2010, The Retirement Report, Moedi

Publishing, Gaborone
25. Letshwene, R.N. 2011, Mastery Over Debt (Audio) Moedi Publishing, Gaborone
26. Letshwene, R.N. 2013, The Savings Report, Moedi Publishing, Gaborone
27. Masterson, M. 2005. Automatic Wealth – the 6 steps to financial independence. New Jersey: John Wiley & Sons Inc.
28. Orman, S. 2001. The Road to Wealth- a comprehensive guide to your money.
29. Orman, S. 2003. The Laws of Money, the lessons of life. New York. Simon & Schuster Inc. (Audio book)
30. Patel, Raj, 2009, The Value of Nothing, Portobello books.
31. Stanley Thomas, J, and Danko William, D, 1996, The Millionaire Next Door, Pocket Books, New York
32. Swart, N.J. 2003, Personal Financial Management, the Southern African guide to personal financial planning, 2nd Edition, Lansdowne: Juta
33. Swart, N.J. 2003, Starting and buying your own business in a franchise, Cape Town: Juta
34. Wilde Stuart, 1989, The Trick to Money is having some!, Hay House, London
35. Hartmann Thom, The Last Hours of Ancient Sunlight, Three Rivers Press, NY, 2004

36. www.Investopedia.com

For More books by Nelson Letshwene:

Scan this:

Or go to:

www.amazon.com/R-Nelson-Letshwene/e/B00Q4AEMCM/ref

www.ingramcontent.com/pod-product-compliance
Lightning Source LLC
Chambersburg PA
CBHW020423220526
45464CB00002B/548